MAGIC EYE III

Visions: A New Dimension in Art

3D Illusions by N.E. Thing Enterprises

Andrews and McMeel
A Universal Press Syndicate Company

Kansas City

ISBN: 0-8362-7017-7

ATTENTION: SCHOOLS AND BUSINESSES

Andrews and McMeel books are available at quantity discounts with bulk purchase for educational, business, or sales promotional use. For information, please write to: Special Sales Department, Andrews and McMeel, 4900 Main Street, Kansas City, Missouri 64112.

INTRODUCTION

He's baaaaack! *Magic Eye III—Visions: A New Dimension in Art* has arrived! Wizzy Nodwig is proud to bring you his latest and greatest 3D illusions!

Those of you who have been clamoring for more have inspired Wizzy to keep the pressure on all of us at N.E. Thing Enterprises to produce another collection of images for your entertainment and amusement. The overwhelming success of *Magic Eye: A New Way of Looking at the World* and *Magic Eye II: Now You See It* . . . is phenomenal, and for that we thank all you loyal gazers!

To those of you who are newcomers, Wizzy says "Welcome!" Once you find your Magic Eye and join us in a new dimension, you will be amazed at what you will discover: images of fantasy and mythical beasts, athletes and monuments . . . all yours for the viewing! All you need to do is practice the simple viewing techniques and you, too, can appreciate this new art form.

3D illusions are a magical blend of artistic expression and computer graphic technology. Thanks to the unlimited creative abilities of the N.E. Thing staff, this art form has no boundaries. You will be seeing our work everywhere, from Wizzy's syndicated comic strip to cereal boxes to clothing. Just look for the Magic Eye logo, and Wizzy will be smiling back at you.

Random dot stereograms have recently been used in editorials involving political satire, and glasses-free viewing was the subject of a Blondie comic strip in which Dagwood was the only one who couldn't see the image. Deep vision is becoming part of our culture, so make sure you jump on the roller coaster and enjoy the ride!

We have all been energized by the outpouring of encouragement. We continue to receive thousands of letters from our readers, or should I say viewers. Every letter is read, and we answer as many as we can. We are most gratified by the letters we receive from children; 3D art has been the focus of many school projects throughout the country and has encompassed many subjects, from art, of course, to science, for perception, to math, for computer codes, to English, for writing business letters, to philosophy, for looking at something from a different point of view. Our books have been translated into nineteen languages, including German, Finnish, Spanish, Hebrew, and Portuguese, and are being distributed worldwide. Our mail has become a philatelist's dream!

Wizzy says we are actually running the national Rorschach test. You'd be amazed to know the incredible variety of items reported to be found in our pictures, most hilarious and some quite strange.

Although our success has been meteoric, we do not rest on our laurels. We continue to work harder than ever to satisfy our loyal fans. A great reward comes from bringing enjoyment to so many with what we do.

Some of the pieces in *Magic Eye III* will challenge your gazing skills even further than before.

Chainsaw Teddy, on page 28, is the embodiment of an ongoing inside joke here at N.E. Thing Enterprises. In early 1994, we produced a really neat poster entitled "Teddy Bear Picnic." The outside image that you see in normal 2D mode was a collage of cute teddy bears, and the inside 3D image was Momma Bear, Poppa Bear, and little Teddy Bear having a picnic. The process of creating the hidden 3D picture resulted in cutting up and scrambling the outside picture. The result was pretty extreme toward the edges of the poster. Cheri Smith, the poster's artist, thought it looked like someone had cut the image up with a chainsaw, and thus we started calling it Chainsaw Teddy. We plan on producing a series of Teddy specials, like "FrankenTeddy" and "Night of the Living Teddies," and "Silence of the Teddies." Let us know what you think!

So, to introduce our cute parody of the monster genre, we introduce Chainsaw Teddy, and on the facing page 29, the disembodied heads of all of us here at N.E. Thing. Sort of a novel way to sneak in a self-portrait. From the top down, in no particular order are: Peggy Baker, librarian; Eric DeWitt, computer systems; Bill Clark, graphics artist; Tom Baccei, founder; Eileen Keneally, creator of Wizzy Nodwig; Sue Thibeault, office manager; Wizzy Nodwig, resident wizard; Andy Paraskevas, artist; Mark Gregorek, agent; Ron Labbe, 3D guru; Irene Earle-Rice, logistics; Lynne Door, mail order manager; Cheri Smith, art director; and Clint Baker, business manager.

The inside back cover endpaper is a puzzle. Nine tubes go from the top of the picture to the bottom. The bottom ends of the tubes are given these letters in order: G, C, M, A, R, D, I, O, and W. Your mission is to follow the tubes from the top to the bottom across the page and write down the letters you find there. The answer will be a magic word.

Many thanks to Jordan Rice, for appearing as the little girl in Visions on page 15.

Remember, no matter how much you think you can see, there's more to be revealed.

VIEWING TECHNIQUES

Learning to use your MAGIC EYE is a bit like learning to ride a bicycle. Once you get it, it gets easier and easier. If possible, try to learn to use your MAGIC EYE in a quiet, meditative time and place. It is difficult for most people to first experience deep vision while otherwise preoccupied in the distracting pinball machine of life. While others teach you, or watch as you try, you're likely to feel foolish and suffer from performance anxiety. Although MAGIC EYE is great fun at work and other entertaining social situations, those are not often the best places to learn. If you don't get it in two or three minutes, wait until another, quieter time. And, if it's hard for you, remember, the brain fairy did not skip your pillow. For most people, it's a real effort to figure out how to use the MAGIC EYE. Almost all of them tell us the effort was well worth it!

In all of the images in MAGIC EYE, you'll note a repeating pattern. In order to "see" a MAGIC EYE picture, two things must happen. First, you must get one eye to look at a point in the image, while the other eye looks at the same point in the next pattern. Second, you must hold your eyes in that position long enough for the marvelous structures in your brain to decode the 3D information that has been coded into the repeating patterns by our computer programs.

There are two methods of viewing our 3D images: Crossing your eyes and diverging your eyes. Crossing your eyes occurs when you aim your eyes at a point between your eyes and an image; diverging your eyes occurs when your eyes are aimed at a point beyond the image.

All of our pictures are designed to be seen by diverging the eyes. It is also possible to see them with the cross-eyed method, but all the depth information comes out backward! (If you try it, we can guarantee that you will not come out backward, too.) If we intend to show an airplane flying in front of a cloud, using the diverging eye method, you will see an airplane-shaped hole cut into the cloud if you look at it with the cross-eyed method. Once you learn one method, try the other. It's fun, but most people do better with one or the other. We think that most people prefer the diverging method.

Another common occurrence is to diverge the eyes twice as far as is needed to see the image. In this case, a weird, more complex version of the intended object is seen. (By the way, if you diverge your eyes while looking at yourself in a mirror, you can find your "third eye" . . . at least we were told that in a letter we received. But you must spend several hours a day looking at yourself in a mirror. Remember, we said it was all right.)

One last note before you start. Although this technique is safe, and even potentially helpful to your eyes, don't overdo it! Straining will not help, and could cause you to feel uncomfortable. That is not the way to proceed. Ask your nephew or the paper girl to give you some help; they'll probably be able to do it in ten seconds. The key is to relax and let the image come to you.

METHOD ONE

Hold the image so that it touches your nose. (Ignore those who might be tempted to make comments about you.) Let the eyes relax, and stare vacantly off into space, as if looking through the image. Relax and become comfortable with the idea of observing the image, without looking at it. When you are relaxed and not crossing your eyes, move the page slowly away from your face. Perhaps an inch every two or three seconds. Keep looking through the page. Stop at a comfortable reading distance and keep staring. The most discipline is needed when something starts to "come in," because at that moment you'll instinctively try to look at the page rather than looking through it. If you look at it, start again.

METHOD TWO

The cover of this book is shiny; hold it in such a way that you can identify a reflection. For example, hold it under an overhead lamp so that it catches its light. Simply look at the object you see reflected, and continue to stare at it with a fixed gaze. After several seconds, you'll perceive depth, followed by the 3D image, which will develop almost like an instant photo!

The last pages of this book provide a key that shows the 3D picture that you'll see when you find and train your MAGIC EYE.

There are some images in the book that do not contain a hidden picture; instead the various repeated objects will seem to float in space at different distances when viewed correctly. These images are on pages 10, 19, 21, 24, 25, and 29. For many, they are easier to see than the other pictures.

We wish you luck, and hope you enjoy this fantastic new art form!

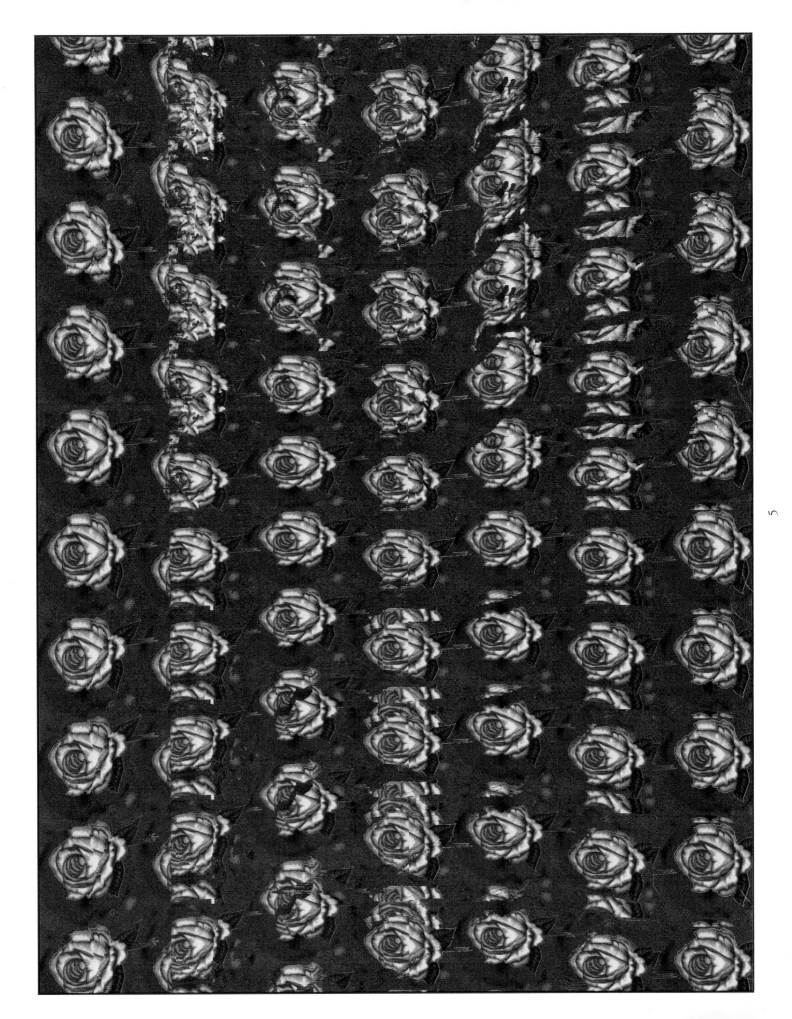

5

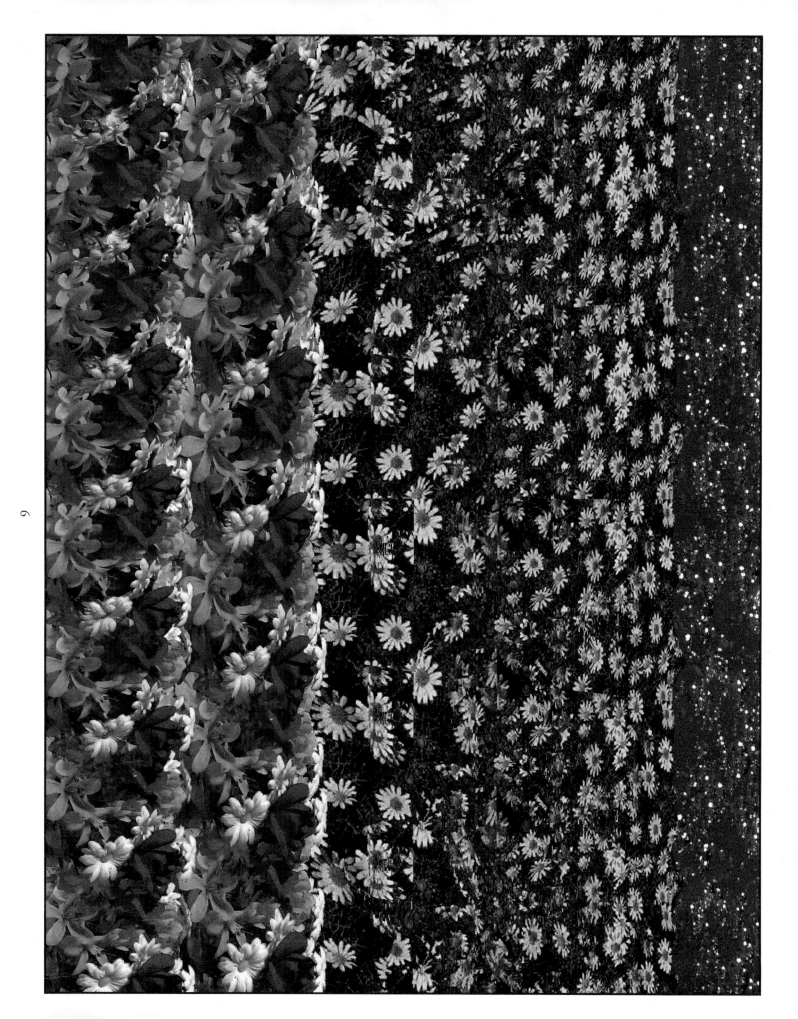

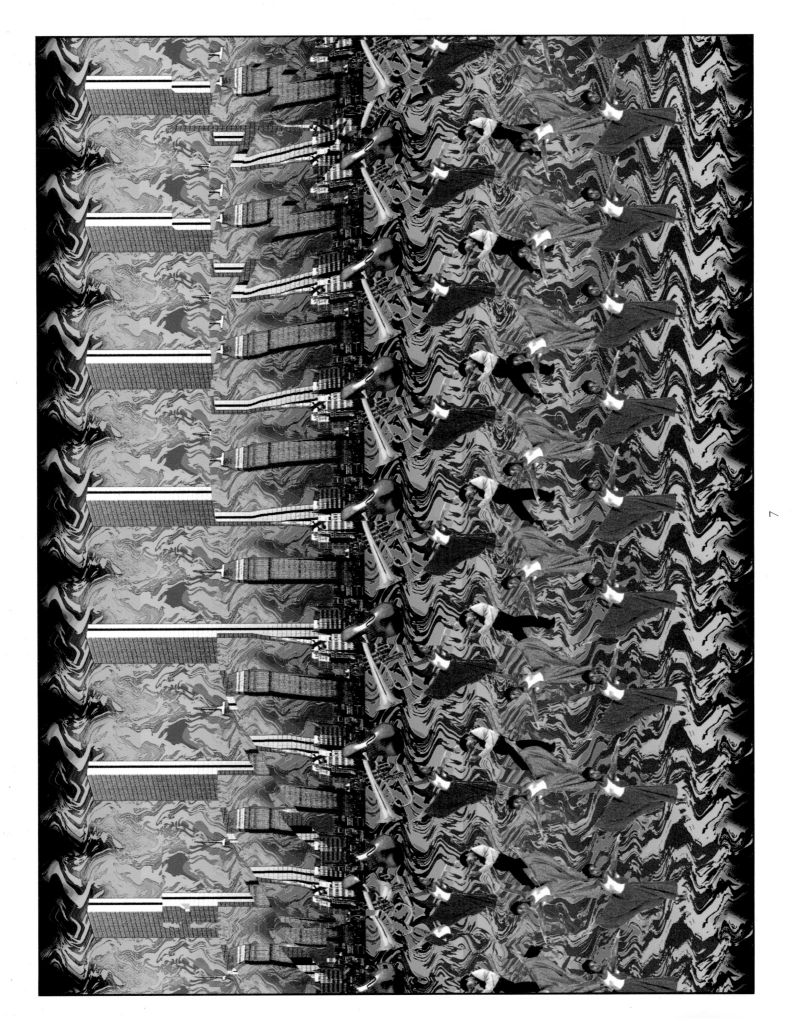

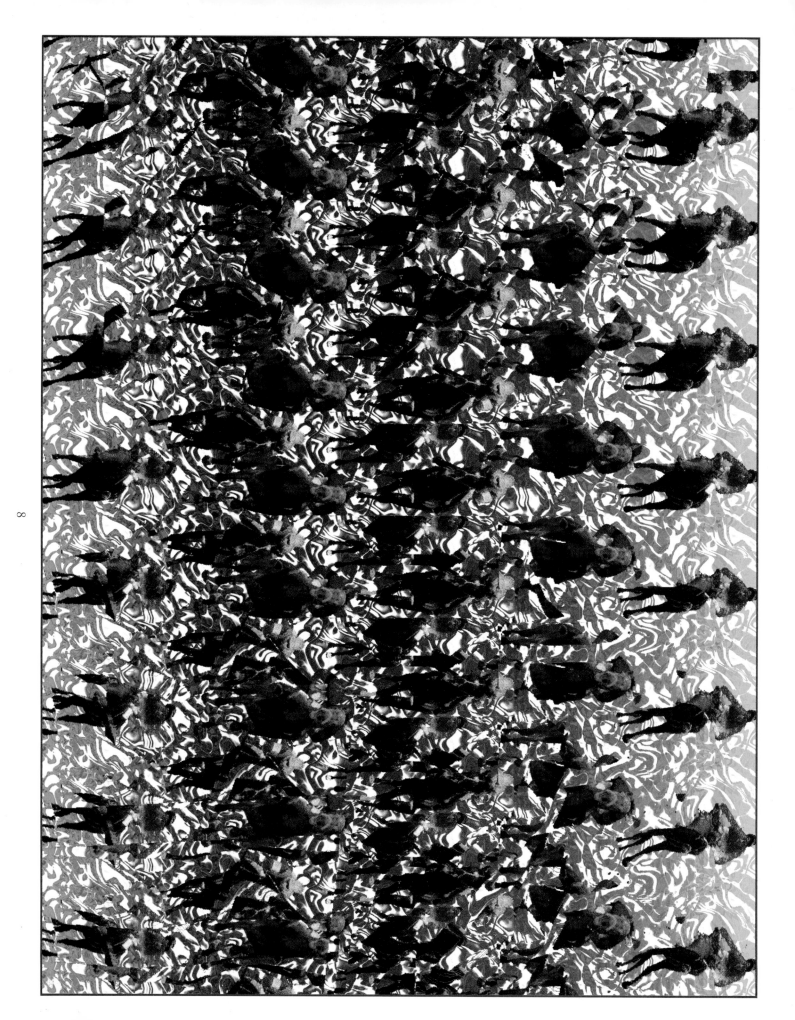

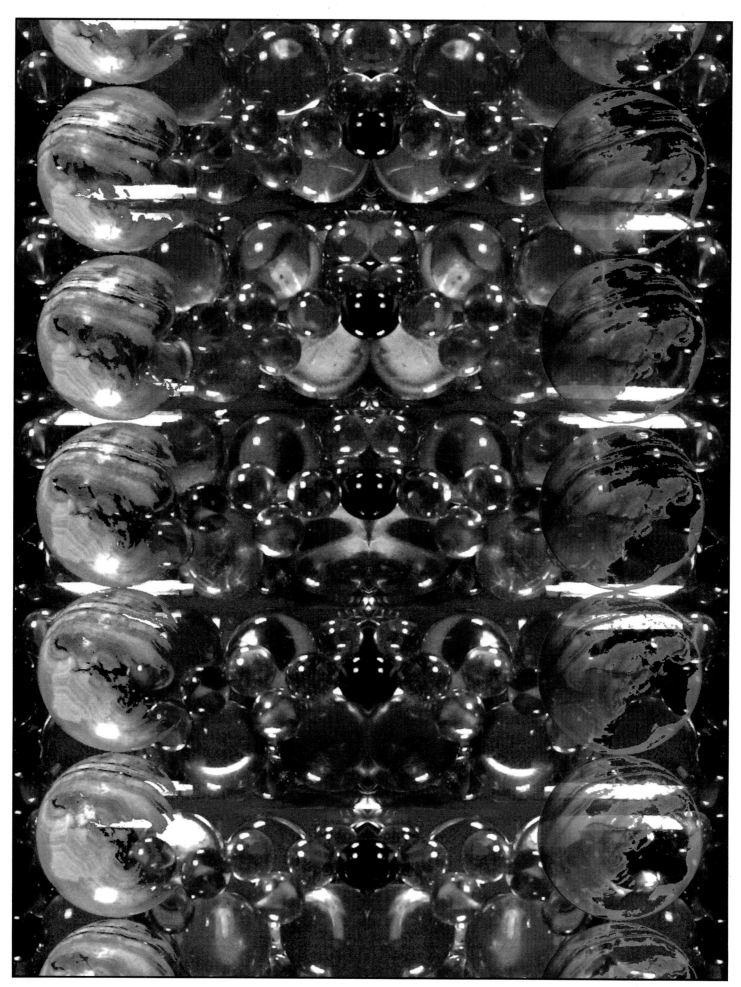

10

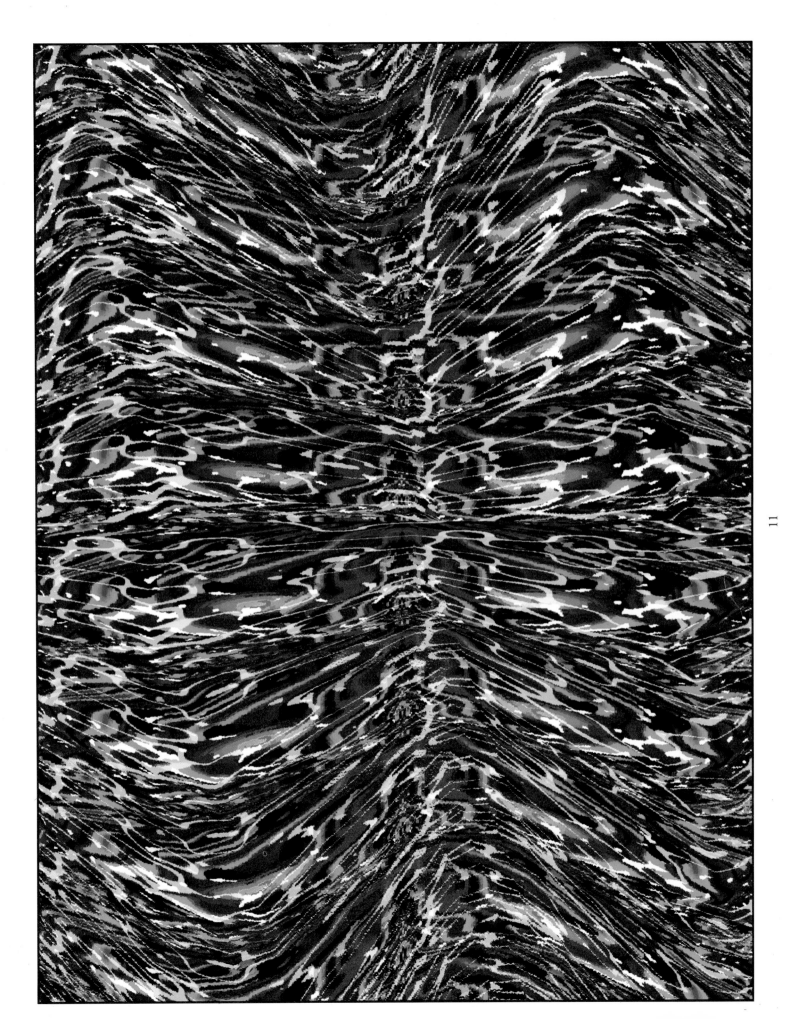

11

12

13

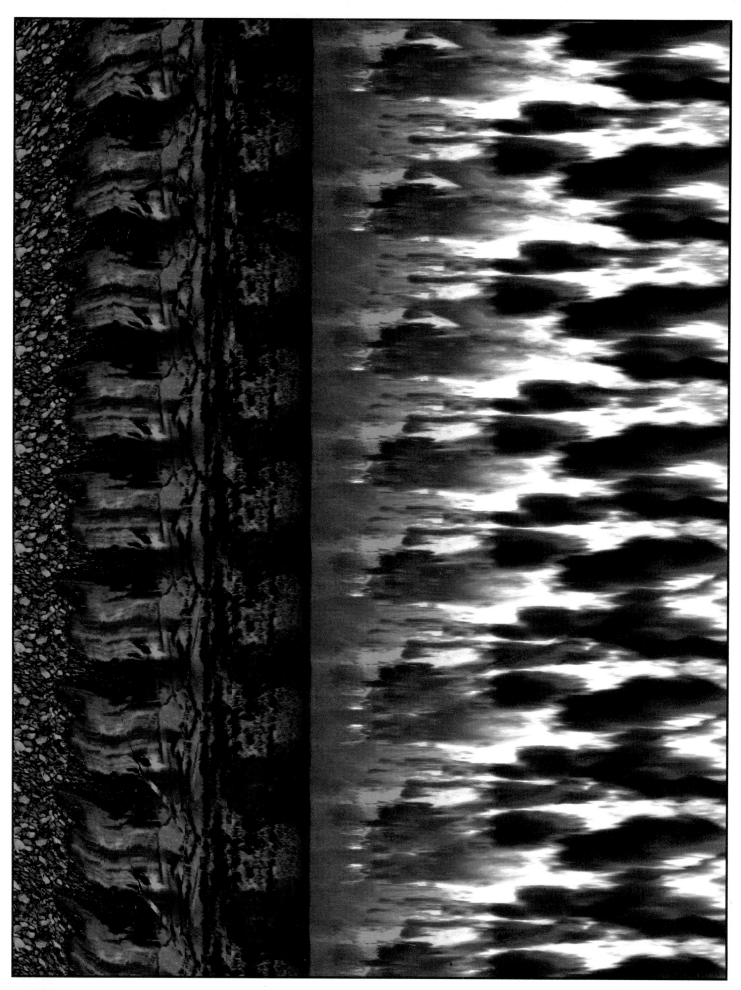

14

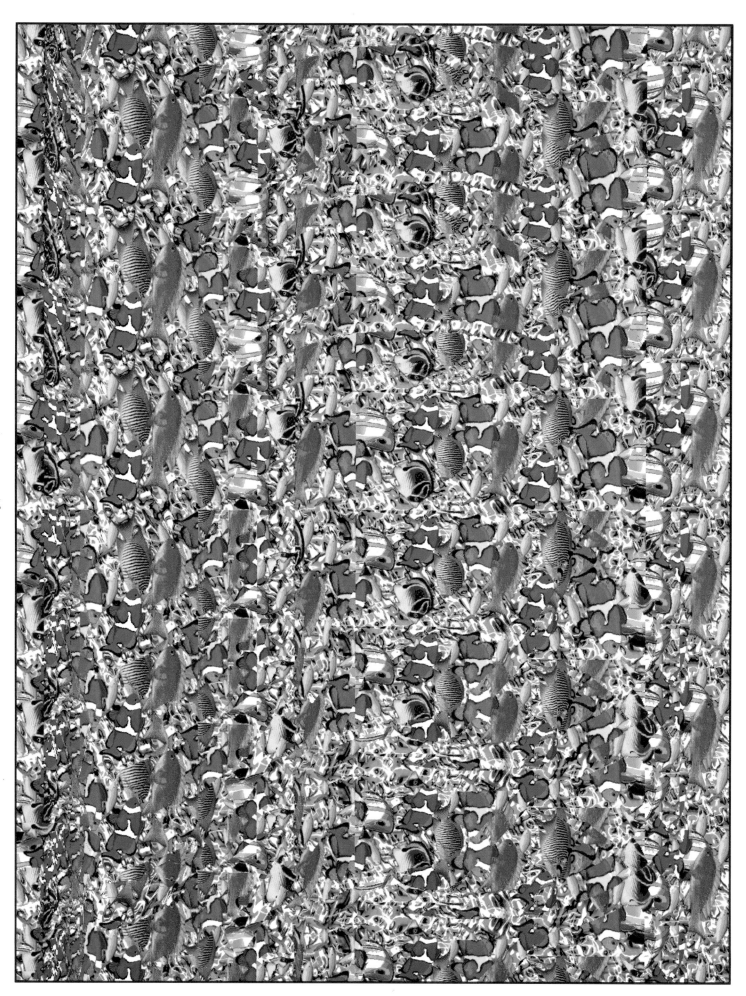

16

18

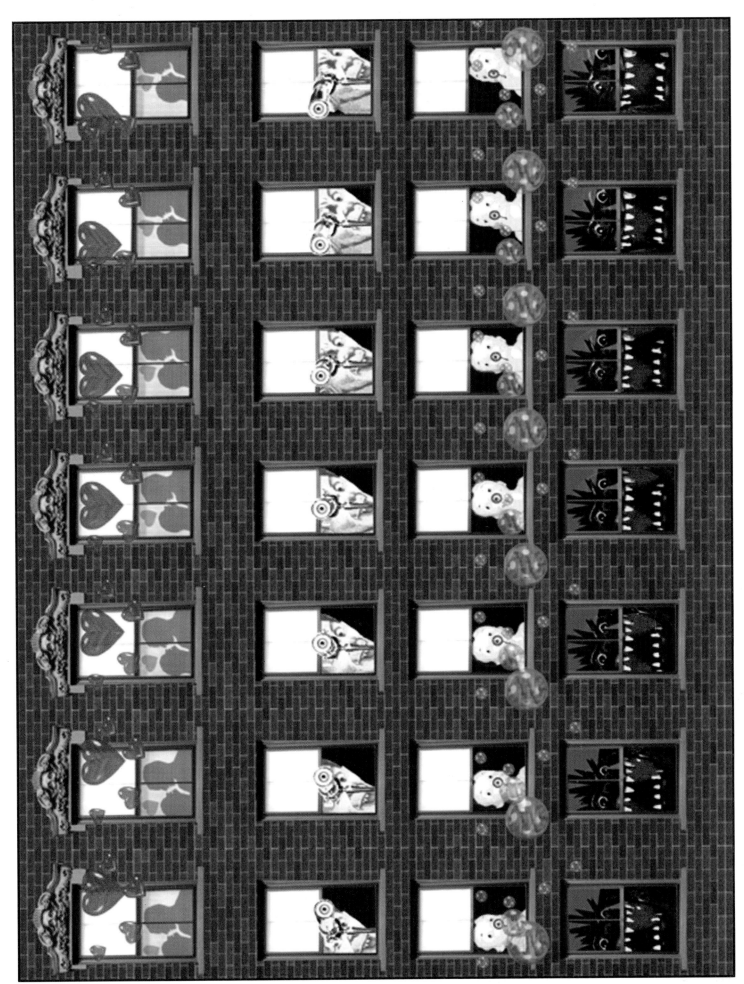

19

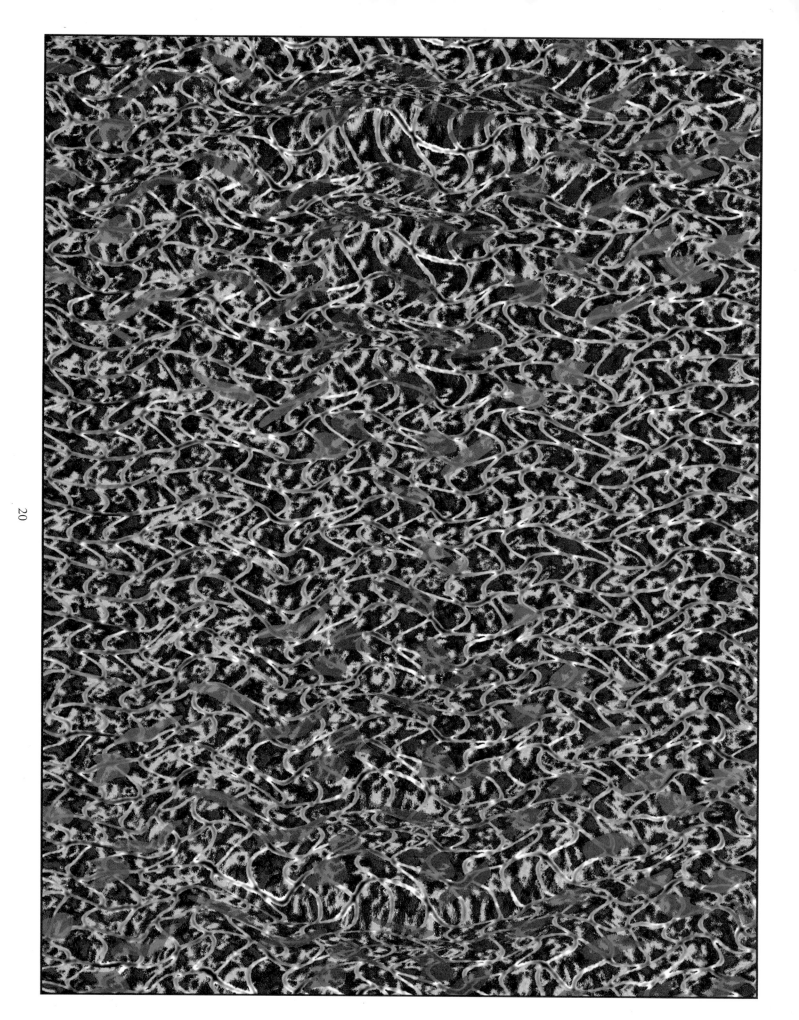

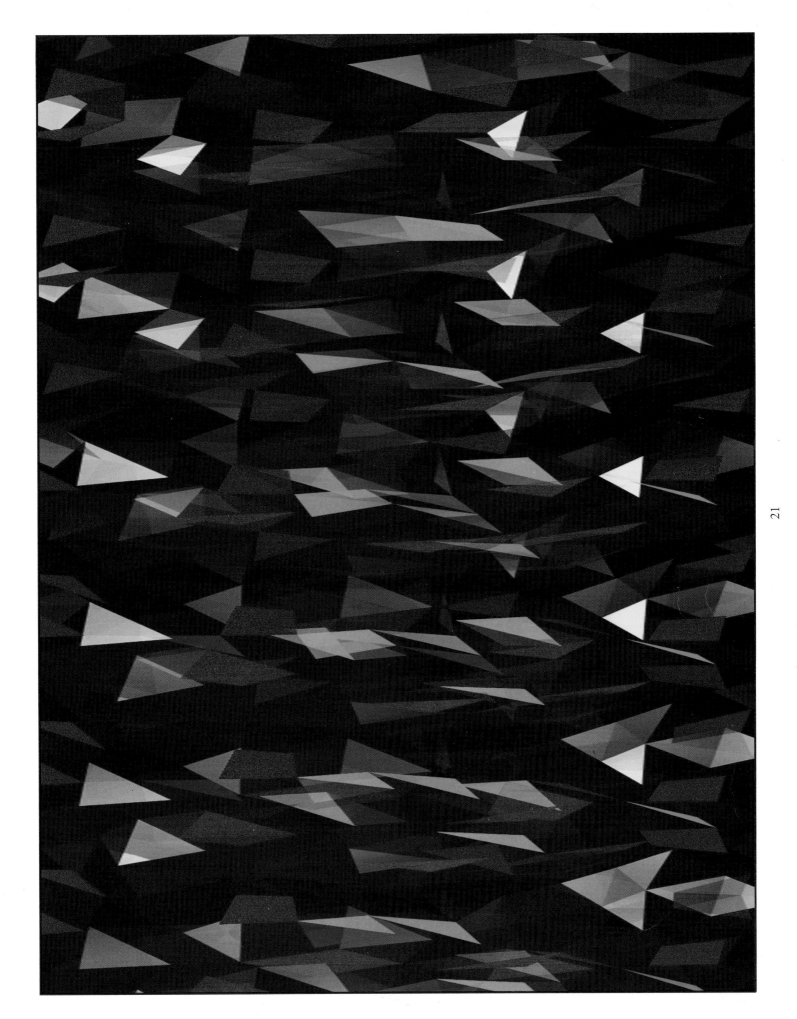

21

22

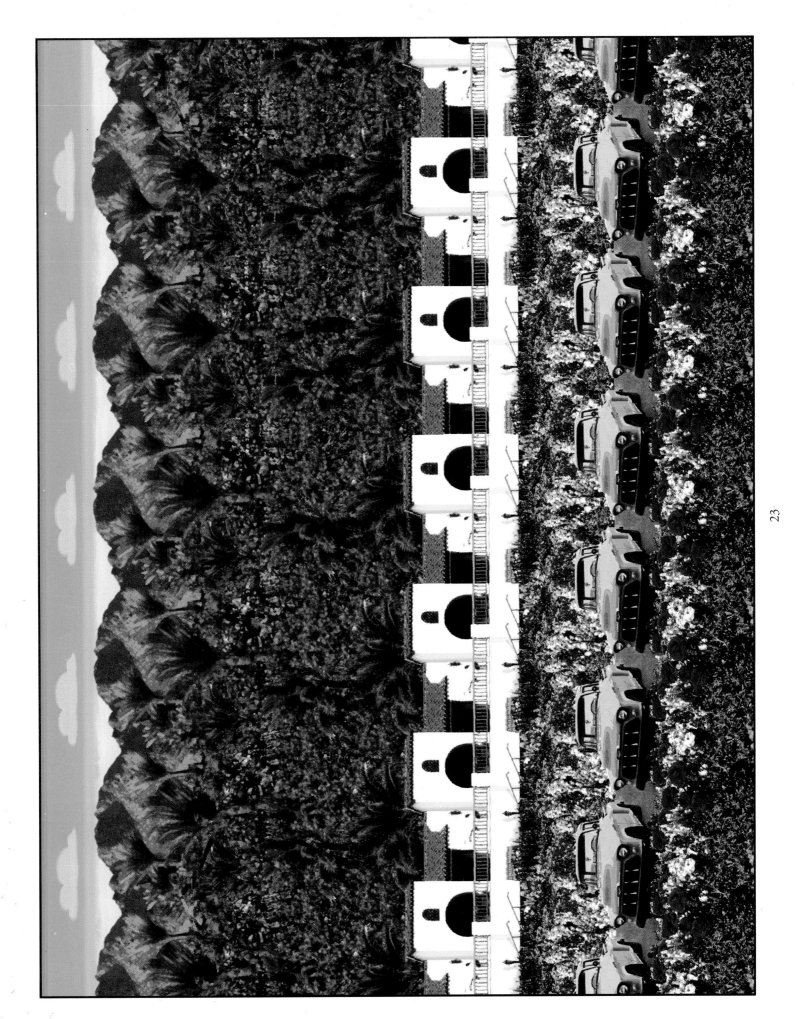

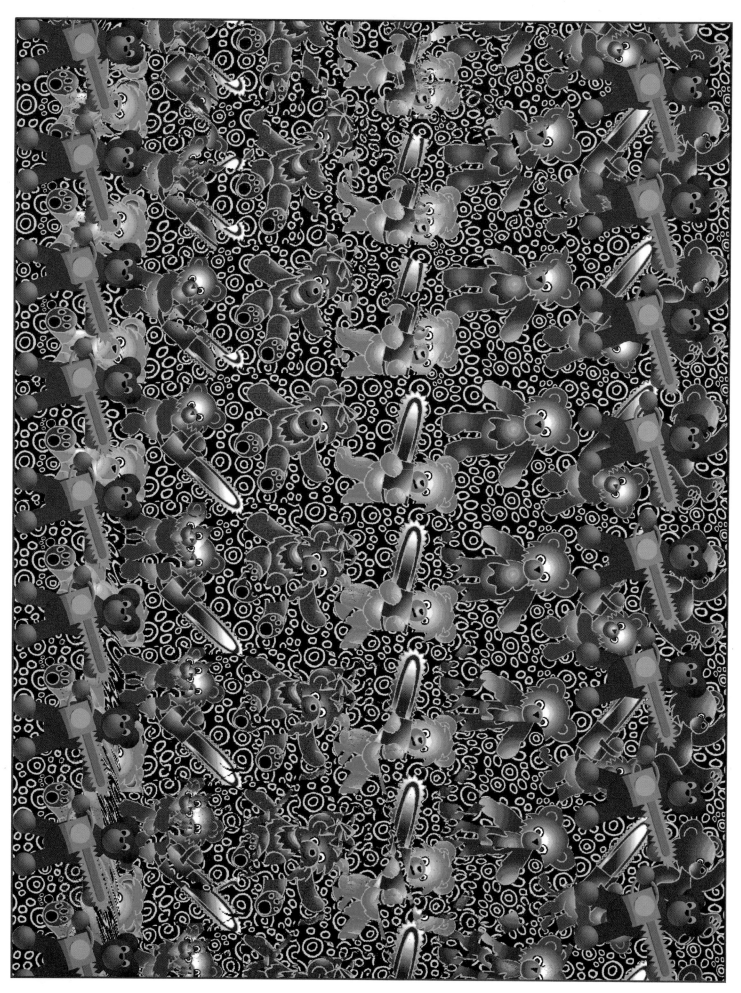

28

Page 6 Tom's Flower III

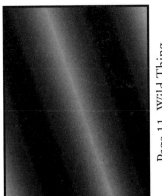

Page 11 Wild Thing

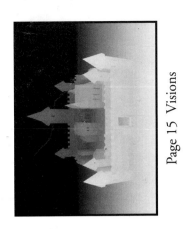

Page 15 Visions

Page 5 Chubby Rub

Page 9 Ruins
Page 10 (No Image)

Page 14 Tidewater

Front Watermark

Page 8 The Stretch

Page 13 RRREX

Page 7 Hatch Shell

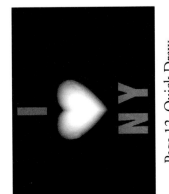

Page 12 Quick Draw

31

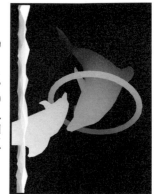

32